PRAISE FOR *JUST FEEL*

"With such a wealth of material from which to pick and choose,
this resource stands out in offering something for everybody. An empowering guide
to finding more satisfaction and calm in life."

—*Kirkus Reviews*, **starred review**

"This engaging guide empowers readers to connect with their emotions
and make positive choices."

—*School Library Journal*

"A useful self-care resource that offers various strategies and balms
for coping with existential growing pains."

—*Publishers Weekly*

PRAISE FOR *JUST BREATHE*

"A solid addition to collections in need of meditation
and mindfulness titles for tweens."

—*School Library Journal*

"Adults sharing mindfulness with children and preteens will find
a treasure trove of scripts for guided practice."

—*Kirkus Reviews*

"I wish I had learned to *Just Breathe* when I was younger. The lessons inside
are priceless, and you will be able to use them for the rest of your life.
All kids—and all adults—should read it."

—**Cara Natterson, pediatrician and *New York Times* best-selling author
of The Care and Keeping of You series**

"*Just Breathe* is the book I wish I had growing up."

—**Tara Stiles, founder of Strala Yoga**

"A charming and engaging book of life skills that speaks directly to tweens
themselves, not through intermediaries like their parents or teachers. Mallika's
wonderful new book is an essential addition to your child's bookshelf!"

—**Susan Kaiser Greenland, author of *Mindful Games* and *The Mindful Child***

JUST
BE YOU

JUST BE YOU

ASK QUESTIONS, SET INTENTIONS, BE YOUR SPECIAL SELF, AND MORE

MALLIKA CHOPRA

author of *Just Breathe* and *Just Feel*

Illustrated by Brenna Vaughan

RP|KIDS
PHILADELPHIA

Running Press Kids
Hachette Book Group
1290 Avenue of the Americas, New York, NY 10104
www.runningpress.com/rpkids
@RP_Kids

Printed in China

First Edition: March 2021

Published by Running Press Kids, an imprint of Perseus Books, LLC,
a subsidiary of Hachette Book Group, Inc. The Running Press Kids name and logo
is a trademark of the Hachette Book Group.

The Hachette Speakers Bureau provides a wide range of authors for speaking events.
To find out more, go to www.hachettespeakersbureau.com or call (866) 376-6591.

The publisher is not responsible for websites (or their content)
that are not owned by the publisher.

Print book cover and interior design by Frances J. Soo Ping Chow.

Library of Congress Control Number: 2020941902

ISBNs: 978-0-7624-7122-5 (paperback), 978-0-7624-7120-1 (ebook)

1010

10 9 8 7 6 5 4 3 2 1

THIS BOOK IS DEDICATED TO YOU, THE READER.

You are the inspiration, the hope,
and the light of the future.
With love,
Mallika

TABLE OF CONTENTS

• • • • •

Why I Wrote This Book . . . xi

Introduction . . . 1

How to Use This Book . . . 2

WHO AM I? . . . 5

Just Be 6

What Makes Me, Me? 8

What Is My Name? 12

Who Is the Real Me? 16

Why Am I Different? 18

Do I Believe in God? 20

What Do My Dreams Mean? 24

What Is My Story? 27

WHAT DO I WANT? . . . 31

What Do I Want? 32

What Are Intentions? 36

What Words Describe Me? 41

Does Anyone See Me? 42

How Do I Deal with Disappointment? 46

How Can I Feel Peaceful? 50

What Symbols Are Meaningful to Me? 54

HOW CAN I SERVE? . . . 59

How Can I Serve? 60

How Can I Take Care of Myself? 63

How Can I Make Good Choices? 67

How Can I Be Kind? 71

What Do I Like to Do? 75

Who Are My Heroes? 76

What Can I Do to Take Care of the Planet? 78

WHAT AM I GRATEFUL FOR? . . . 83

Who Am I Grateful For? 85

What Are My Favorite Holidays? 89

What Inspires Me? 90

Gratitude for Life Itself! 92

What Did It Take for This Moment to Happen? 96

What Do I See When I Look at a Flower? 98

Afterword by Deepak Chopra . . . 105

Resources . . . 106

Acknowledgments . . . 107

WHY I WROTE THIS BOOK

Hello, I am Mallika. My full name is Mallika Chopra.

I am a mom and an author. My husband's name is Sumant, and our daughters' names are Tara and Leela. Our dog's name is Yoda. He is lazy, but very friendly and cute.

I am Indian American. I grew up in Boston, Massachusetts, and now live in Santa Monica, California.

Sumant and I got married a long time ago in India. We had a traditional wedding with hundreds of people invited—it lasted for a week! In our family, when a woman gets married, she wears red and lots of jewelry. I felt like a princess at my wedding.

I love to walk by the ocean near my house in California. I love to plan trips to different places, especially when it is with my family and friends.

I like to read good stories. And I like to get together with my friends to talk about books we all really enjoyed reading.

Sometimes I spend way too much time playing video games, and my daughter needs to take them off my computer so I can do work.

I love to go to concerts. And I really, *really* like chocolate chip cookies, but, for my health, I am trying to eat less of them.

Although I speak to large audiences and teach kids in classrooms, I am actually quite shy and feel awkward when I'm in big groups of people.

I am happiest when I am at home with my family.

These are just a few things about me that I wanted to share with you. There are other things that I tend to keep private, like my fears and insecurities and what makes me sad.

In this book, I hope that you will learn more about who you are, what you like best, and what makes you feel most happy and peaceful. Also, I hope that it helps you think about who you *want* to be—by knowing and celebrating what is unique and amazing about just being you!

INTRODUCTION

This book will hopefully help you to learn more about yourself, what makes you happy, and how to shape who you want to be.

Until now, your parents or other adults have probably decided a lot of things about your life: your name, where you live, what furniture is in your home, and the clothes you wear. They probably influence what you do and who you are around by choosing your extracurricular activities or setting up playdates or summer camps for you. Or you may participate in whatever activities are available to you in school or at your community center, because that is easiest for your family.

Right now, your friends may be people who live in your apartment complex, are on your sports team, or are in your class at school.

But if you are old enough to be reading this book—on your own, in your classroom, at the library, or with an adult—you are at a stage in your life where you can begin to reflect on your values, your talents, what you love to do, and who you want to be around. You are old enough to start making some decisions for yourself about all those things.

You are also old enough to start setting intentions for your life. Intentions are what you want deep down inside and include:

* who you want to be

* who you want to be around

* how you want to feel

* how you want to treat others
and be treated

* what you want to do

* what you want to achieve

* what you want to do for others

* what you want to do for your world

Adults who love you are there to guide and support you. Parents, teachers, mentors, friends, and others can influence what you do every day, what you study, and how you organize your extracurricular activities, and they can help you think about what you could be when you grow up.

Ultimately, though, *you* set your intentions. *You* can decide who you want to become, who you interact with and learn from, how hard you work, and what happiness and success mean to you.

The journey of being *just you* is full of twists and turns, ups and downs, fulfillment and lots of adventure. It's a ride I hope you'll enjoy!

HOW TO USE THIS BOOK

This book asks you a lot of questions. It will:

• ask you to think about who you are and
what makes you special

• help you reflect on the type of person you wish to be

• show you how to set intentions for
what you want to achieve

• guide you to serve yourself and
those you love with pride

Don't worry if you can't answer some of the questions—either now or later. And it's important to know that your answers to these questions will keep changing throughout your life. That is natural and normal.

The goal of this book is to help you just *be*.

Remember: We are human be-ings, not human do-ings.

If you are guided by who you want to be, then you will choose to do things to make your goals happen. You'll make choices based on what makes you feel happy, and when you take action, you'll feel that what you're doing is meaningful. The hope of this book is to teach you to always ask questions and to learn to live out the answers.

Living your questions makes life interesting, challenging, and fulfilling!

"Be patient toward all that is unsolved in your heart and try to *love the questions themselves* like locked rooms and like books that are written in a very foreign tongue. *Live* the questions now. Perhaps you will then gradually, without noticing it, live along some distant day into the answer."
—RAINER MARIA RILKE

WHO AM I?

Just Be

• • • • •

As you begin this book, take a moment to *just be*. Take a deep breath—in and out. Appreciate this very moment. Look around you. Feel your body. Breathe in and out again.

EXERCISE:
BEING

- - - - - - - - - - - -

Time Needed: **ONE MINUTE**
Location: **WHEREVER YOU ARE JUST NOW**

Before you start the following exercise, either read or listen to someone else read the directions, and then put the book down while you do the exercise. If you are reading this with an adult or with your class, you can all do the exercise together.

Put aside the book, as well as anything else that may distract you. Turn off the TV or video games, close your computer screen, silence any music you are listening to, and set aside your phone, turning it to silent mode.

Sitting exactly where you are and with your eyes open, look straight ahead and take a deep breath, in and out.

Just breathe. In and out.

Notice what is happening in your body as you breathe in and out.

Now notice what is happening around you when you are doing nothing.

Again, breathe in and out.

How does it feel to just be you? Just be-ing.

Take another breath, in and out.

Now go back to whatever you were do-ing.

The purpose of this exercise is to remind you that no matter what you are doing, *you* are the one doing it.

As you read or listen to these words, take a deep breath and notice that you are the one having this experience.

You are the one in your body.

You are the one thinking.

You are always there when you take that deep breath, in and out.

What Makes Me, Me?

• • • • •

You Are Your Body.

Different parts of your body—inside and outside—work together to make you live.

Your heart beats inside of you, pumping blood throughout your body. If you sit still, can you feel how your heart has its own rhythm?

Your stomach digests the food you eat, and other organs like the kidney, liver, and colon help you clean out any inside waste to feel better.

Notice how you can sense how your body feels just by putting your attention on different parts of it. When you breathe in deeply, you can feel your lungs get bigger, bringing in oxygen to give you energy. Take a deep breath right now, and notice how, when you bring in air, your body naturally lets air out as well.

You can understand your body and learn how to take care of it in a way that is best for you.

Perhaps you have a physical disability, and you are learning how to use your body to live well. You may use a wheelchair or crutches or some other support to help you move around.

It could be that your body is struggling on the inside, even though no one can see it. You may have pain, a hard time breathing, or dangerous allergies to certain foods, or you may be going through treatment that you choose to share or to keep private from others in your life. You may be more aware of your body than others because you are focused on survival.

Learning to know your unique physical body, and what it needs to be healthy, is important for you to feel independent and strong as you get older.

You Are Your Mind.

You have thoughts, feelings, and beliefs. You take in the world with your five senses: seeing, hearing, smelling, tasting, and touching. Some of your senses may feel more powerful than others. For example, you may learn best by hearing a teacher tell you a story, while your friend may learn the same thing better when they see pictures on a page.

All your experiences—and the experiences of those around you—have shaped how you view yourself and the world. Sometimes, especially as you get older, you may realize that you experience the world differently than your family, friends, teachers, or others in your community. And that's perfectly all right.

You Are Your Creativity.

You can use your body and mind to express yourself and just be you!

You can use your words, move your body, draw a picture, and make music in a way that no one else can.

Your creativity comes from inside of you, but also from a place that often feels bigger than you. Different people experience the source of creativity and inspiration in different ways. There may even be times when you are surprised by what you create! You may think, *How did I do that?*

Remember that when you express yourself, there is nothing good or bad about it. *It just is.* It is special and unique and your own magic.

THREE BREATHS (FOR BODY, MIND, AND CREATIVITY)

Time Needed: **ONE MINUTE**
Location: **ANYWHERE**

This exercise helps you connect with the different parts of you: your body, your mind, and that place from which creativity inspires you. You will be taking three deep breaths in this exercise for each of those parts of you.

Sit comfortably.

Close your eyes if you are comfortable doing so. If you feel better keeping your eyes open, that is okay.

Put one hand on your stomach and your other hand on your heart (whichever hand feels most comfortable is all right).

Take a deep breath, in and out.

Say, "My body."

Move your hands to your face, and place your fingers over your eyes, letting your hands feel your cheeks and your palms feel comfortable on your jaw.

Take a second deep breath, in and out.

Say, "My mind."

Now move your hands down to the sides of your body.

Shift your attention, outside of your body, to the space around you. Feel the air around you, the openness of the space above your head.

Take a third deep breath, in and out.

Say, "My creativity."

Open your eyes if they were closed. Take one last breath, in and out.

AMIRA Madeline Xavier Celia Yoshi TOBEY
Keshawn Aditya Izzy Mei Abigail Malik
Caliegh Ahyoka Landon Wyatt JASMINE Max
FRANCES Tiara Ahmad Jose Logan Andre
Sofia Aniya Juan Ben Deja ABDUL Kate
AUSTIN Luke Valentina Terrell Samir JALEN
Uri Cody Emily DIAMOND Hunter Farrah

What Is My Name?

• • • • •

On a piece of paper, write the following:

My name is _____ _____ _____.
(Fill in the blanks.)

Maybe you have a middle name or a hyphenated last name or several last names. Thinking about your name can give you insight into how you and others may think about who you are. Your name may reflect a lot about you, or it may lead people to make assumptions about you that aren't true.

Here are some questions to think about when you are considering your name and how you present yourself to others. Note: there are no right or wrong questions here; rather, thinking about these things can help you learn more about yourself.

• Do you use a nickname instead of
your given name? Why?

• What does your last name tell you and others
about your family?

• Are you named after someone?

• Who gave you your name?

• What does your name mean?

*• How many other people do you know who have
the same first name as you? Or the same last name?
Do you share anything in common with them?*

In different cultures, there are different ways that people name their children. Some use names of important people in their religious tradition. Some spend a lot of time thinking about the qualities they want in their children and name them after those. For some families, it is important to keep traditions alive through names, and so they repeat names on purpose.

In some cultures, people don't name their kids until the babies reveal more about their personality. And often some names are more popular during a certain time period because there was a person who that society respected.

As you think about your name, know that you have the power to embrace the essence and history that comes from it, but also the power to not let your name simply define you.

A character in a play by William Shakespeare says, "What's in a name? That which we call a rose by any other name would smell as sweet." What do you think? Do you agree with this statement?

EXERCISE:
CREATE A NAME FOR YOURSELF

Time Needed: **HOWEVER LONG YOU WANT**
Location: **ANYWHERE**

Think about who you aspire to be—whether it is the qualities you wish to demonstrate in your life or the roles you want to play in your community. Think of objects or adjectives that represent these qualities.

Perhaps it is an object in nature like the grandness and expanse of branches of a tree on your street or the flowing water in a river near where you live. It could be the changing shapes of a cloud or the sounds of an owl outside your window at night.

Or perhaps it is qualities like kindness, love, gratitude, strength, insight.

Create a name for yourself that represents the power, wisdom, and strength you want in your life.

You can keep this private, as something that is just yours. Or share the name with someone you trust, and tell them why you chose it.

You may want to draw a picture that represents your desired name or even write a song or poem that captures all the things you appreciate about it.

In some Native American cultures, leaders and members of the community are initiated with a new name when they demonstrate power, wisdom, or strength. These names are often inspired by nature, like the names Sitting Bull and Red Cloud.

Who Is the Real Me?

· · · · ·

Your life is influenced by many things: your family, race, religion, and nationality; where you live; and how much money your family has. You may feel judged by others by the way you look, by your gender and race, or by the clothes or shoes you wear.

Deep down inside, you may feel different from the labels that people put on you. For example, others may see you as a boy or girl. But you may feel differently. Some kids look like one gender, but they realize they don't fit the definition of how others see them.

People may see you as Black, white, Asian, Hispanic, or mixed race. But you may identify instead with a specific culture, religion, or country.

You may say:

- I am Puerto Rican. I am Japanese. I am Punjabi.
  I am Persian. I am French.
- I am Indian and Chinese American.
- My parents came from Guatemala, but I am from California.
  I am Hispanic American.
- I am Muslim. I am Christian. I am Jewish.
  I am a Hindu. I am Zoroastrian.

You may come from a big family, or you may be an only child. You may always be seen as the little sister or the middle child. And, because of this, people may treat you differently from how they treat your siblings.

You may be homeless or live in a foster home. When others find out, they may make assumptions about your happiness or what you can accomplish.

You may be an athlete or musician or dancer or martial artist. You may be known as a nerd or a jock or the popular kid. Maybe you feel as if no one even knows *who* you are. Depending on the role you play at school, other kids may treat you in a certain way.

Always remember that you are more than what others assume about you. Don't let anyone else put limits on what you can do, how you think, or how you want to express yourself.

The real *you* is the one who takes their unique life circumstances and then questions, explores, pushes, and strives to be their best.

Why Am I Different?

• ◦ • ◦ •

You are different from everyone else in the world.

You look different from others. It may be the color of your skin or your eyes, the texture of your hair, your weight, or your height.

You sound different, too. The sound of your voice, your accent, or how you use language is yours alone.

You move in a way that is unique to you. You have your own way of walking, running, and dancing. You may have a physical disability. Your posture and physical presence are unique.

You make different choices in what you eat, what you wear, what music you listen to, and what you choose to do with your time.

Even if you are a twin or triplet (quadruplet or quintuplet!), you know that you are your own unique person.

Your thoughts are your own, and you choose how to express yourself.

Always remember: Differences make the world vibrant, fun, and interesting!

You may feel nervous about sharing your thoughts and feelings with others because you feel differently from how they feel. You may be scared that people will get mad or not love you the same way if you share how you are really feeling. Remember: even if you feel different, others are different too. There are people in this world who will appreciate your differences—you just may need to find them.

Sometimes it can feel really lonely and scary to be different. Perhaps you:

• are the only person of color in your school

• speak a different language at home than your friends

• think you are the only gay person in your class

• are the only girl on the school robotics team

• come from a family that doesn't have as much money
as everyone else you know

Sadly, sometimes differences are used as a reason to bully people and make them feel excluded or ashamed.

If someone is teasing you about your differences, it can be very difficult in the moment to remember that they are probably doing this because they are scared themselves. Only the weak bully others, and only those who are insecure about who they are tease others. Try to find a trusted adult—maybe even someone outside your family—to confide in if you are feeling scared about expressing your differences and especially if you feel threatened by anyone.

If you are the one suspicious of someone else because they are different, ask yourself why you feel this way. Take a moment to realize that you will be stronger and more interesting if you learn their story and become their friend and ally.

Try to shift feelings about being different to celebrate the uniqueness of you and others in your life! You can find different ways to process your feelings. Perhaps it is writing a song or painting or dancing. Or you can explore theater or poetry, playing an instrument, or drumming to express what's inside of you.

Do I Believe in God?

• ◦ • ◦ •

Different families believe different things.

Most kids, particularly when they are young, believe in the same God or practice the same religion as their parents. Some families don't believe in God—perhaps they believe in a higher power or enveloping spirit that connects all of us, or maybe they don't believe in anything spiritual.

People in your community may practice a similar religion and share common rituals. Perhaps you meet others at church, temple, synagogue, or mosque on a daily or weekly basis.

For others, your family may be one of the few that practice your religion where you live. This may make you feel very different from your friends, but maybe it makes you feel more connected to your family, too.

There are many families that practice a certain religion but don't regularly go somewhere to practice it. They may incorporate a spiritual practice at home and prefer to keep their religious beliefs private.

As you grow older, you may begin to question your family's beliefs in God or spirituality. This can be difficult because you may feel scared that people will get angry with you if you waver from the family's tradition.

A great way to connect with your grandparents, parents, and religious and community leaders is to ask about religion and beliefs and learn why there are certain rituals that people practice. By asking questions, you will invite these people to pass on personal, cultural, and community stories to you that might help you make a decision about what you want to believe.

Here are some questions you may want to explore on your own or with trusted adults in your life:

• Do you pray? If so, to whom?

• Why do you pray?

• Do you pray once a day, five times a day, on holidays,
or whenever you remember? Why?

• What does "God" mean to you?

• Why do we have certain rituals?
(baptism, *quinceañera*, bar and bat mitzvah)

Some kids may not feel comfortable talking to family or religious leaders about these questions, as it feels disrespectful to question things. If this is the case, pay attention to how those around you use religion, prayer, or rituals to help them get through life. You can learn a lot through watching others, reading, and seeing how your family's practice makes you feel connected to a larger community.

LEARN ABOUT RELIGIONS

- - - - - - - - - - -

Time Needed: **AS MUCH AS YOU WANT—EVEN A LIFETIME!**
Location: **ANYWHERE**

The major religions of the world are Christianity, Islam, Hinduism, Buddhism, Sikhism, and Judaism.

Jainism, Baha'i, and Zoroastrianism are also practiced by many around the world.

Taoism, Shinto, and Confucianism influence philosophy and traditions particularly in Asia.

In Africa, there are many rituals and local beliefs that are part of everyday life and have become part of the rituals of other religions.

Many Native Americans and other indigenous people (in Australia, Asia, and South America) see spirit in all aspects of the earth and animals and have divine respect for all things.

Some of the most well-known people in different religions are:

- *Jesus Christ*
- *the Virgin Mary*
- *Moses*
- *the Prophet Muhammad*
- *Buddha*
- *Guru Nanak*
- *Confucius*

Take time to learn about the philosophies and people of different religions. Ask parents, teachers, and religious leaders in your community to share stories. There is so much to learn!

You can form your own beliefs and connect with others who are different from you with knowledge and respect.

Who Am I?

What Do My Dreams Mean?

· · · · ·

When you sleep, your body and mind get the very important rest that helps you stay healthy and grow so that you can be your best self. When you sleep, you process all that you learned and experienced during the day.

And, of course, you dream!

Dreams are like going into a different world, where your imagination takes over. Sometimes your dreams feel like real life with a twist, and sometimes they are super random and seem to have nothing to do with you. Often, your dream feels so real that it's only once you wake up that you realize you were simply dreaming.

You may feel as if you have the same dream over and over again, or you may never be able to remember your dreams. Making a conscious effort to remember your dreams every morning can be a fun, and even insightful, practice. You may find that your dreams are trying to tell you something.

Perhaps in the crazy story line of a dream where your best friend struggles to climb up a giant purple ladder, you understand that your friend needs a helping hand. Or if in your dream there is a rabbit playing a piano, it may somehow remind you of your grandmother (who loves to play the piano), and you decide to call her. You might have a nightmare about your favorite teddy bear being in trouble, and it reminds you to sleep with him again.

You can choose how much you want to interpret your dreams. If you are having fun with it, dream interpretation can be a way to fuel your imagination, especially for art, music, and stories.

EXERCISE:

DREAM JOURNAL

Time Needed: A FEW MINUTES EVERY MORNING
Location: IN YOUR BEDROOM
Materials Needed: A JOURNAL OR SEVERAL PIECES OF PAPER

Try this exercise for a week.

When you wake up in the morning, before jumping out of bed, pause, take a deep breath, and with your eyes closed, see if you can remember what you dreamed about that night.

You may not remember anything—that is okay. Sometimes it takes a while and a conscious effort to get used to remembering your dreams.

On those days when you do remember your dream, write down what you remember. You can write down the story of your dream if you remember it. Or if you just remember images, draw or write them down.

If you just have a feeling when you wake up, you can write that down as well.

If you are unsure if something was actually in your dream, don't worry if it was or wasn't; just include it in your journal.

At the end of the week, review your notes. See if they mean anything to you. Maybe they are telling you to solve a problem, reach out to someone, or try something new. Or maybe they are just fun and inspire you to draw, sing, dance, or tell someone a story.

What Is My Story?

• • • • •

Right now, you have a unique story that is yours alone.

It may be a story you feel really good about, or it may be one that has parts, even lots of parts, that you want to change completely.

Your story today may be very different from what it was last year. And your story a year from now can change depending on things that may happen that are beyond your control. Life and situations keep changing, but you can influence your story depending on what you choose to focus on and how you choose to act.

There is power in knowing your story, because when you know yourself, and what makes you happy or frustrated, unsafe or powerful, you can feel in control and more confident of who you want to be.

Let's start to discover your story.

The first step in telling your story is to think about the things in your life that are fairly constant. This *may* be your name, your sex, the people around you, and the places you physically spend time in, like your home or school. For some, these may change (or be changing) and not be reliable parts of who you are. Remember, though, that the change itself is part of your story.

Your story also includes what you do every day, your likes and dislikes, your friends and the other people you interact with, and what you are reading or singing or playing.

As you think about these things, ask yourself, if they changed, would you still be the same inside?

If you are confused about your story, it's okay. Lots of people are, and life is a process of discovering and creating your story.

Simply take a deep breath.

Remember that feeling of just be-ing?

No matter what may change in your life, you can always go back to that feeling as your constant *you*.

WHAT'S MY STORY TODAY?

- - - - - - - - - - -

Time Needed: **AS LONG AS YOU WANT,
AND OVER AND OVER AGAIN!**
Location: **ANYWHERE**
Materials Needed: **PAPER, PAINT, CRAYONS**

Everyone expresses their story differently.

Some like to speak or sing. Others prefer to write or draw. And some simply want to dance.

In whatever form you wish, express today's story. You could start with your name, where you live, what you like or dislike, what you've been doing today, or what you are planning to do later. You may even want to include a dream from the previous night or a goal for what you wish to be in the future (these too are part of who you are today).

Be honest with yourself when it comes to what you feel good about, and when something arises that may feel uncomfortable, take a deep breath and go back to the feeling of be-ing.

Remember that you are the one telling this story.

If you chose to waver into an imaginary space with your story, go for it! Part of creating a life you want is including the magic that you want to feel inside. Your imagination can help you feel it today.

You get to choose the words, colors, actions, feelings, and memories to be a part of your story.

You are the perfect and only storyteller for your unique story!

WHAT DO I WANT?

What Do I Want?

· · · · ·

If you had to write a list of what you want in your life, what would be on it?

Things people want normally include physical things or experiences. Perhaps your list includes toys, clothes, sneakers, books, or video games. Or it could include attending a basketball game or a concert by your favorite musician. It could be that you want to take a trip to visit your grandparents or do something super special like going skiing in the mountains or surfing in Hawaii.

You may want different things than your siblings or friends, because you have your own unique interests.

It is important to think about *why* you want what you want, because sometimes you may find yourself wanting things that other people have so that you don't feel left out. Often, when you finally get those things, you may not feel as fulfilled because you were actually wishing for something more personal to you.

Remember that every person has different circumstances that lead them to get the things they want. Your family may have limited resources and need to spend money on the place where you live, on food, or on supporting someone's health instead of buying things.

You may want a certain pair of sneakers that your friend has, but you know that your family has no way to buy them for you. Instead of feeling angry about this, you can reflect on why that pair of sneakers is something you want and then get some insight into your priorities as you grow older and are spending money. If you had limited money, would that pair of sneakers give you more happiness than anything else?

Knowing what you want can be a powerful motivator to do well in school and to work hard down the road. And if there is a thing or experience you want so badly, think about what you can do to support others in your life to make it happen.

What Do I Want?

ASK SOMEONE YOU LOVE WHAT THEY WANT

- - - - - - - - - - - - - - - -

Time Needed: FIVE MINUTES
Location: ANYWHERE

Choose someone you love and trust in your life. This could be a parent, grandparent, sibling, cousin, friend, teacher, or mentor. They can be older or younger than you.

Ask this person one simple question: What do you want?

See if they say material things, experiences, or connections to other people.

Learning about what others want can help you learn more about them. It may also give you ideas of how you can support someone you love by helping them get what they truly want.

What Are Intentions?

· · · · ·

One way of thinking about what you want is to think about how you want to feel physically and emotionally, and the kind of relationships you hope to have. These are called your desires.

Here is a list of common desires:

- I want to feel healthy.
- I want a loving family.
- I want meaningful friendships.
- I want to feel confident in my abilities.
- I want my family to be financially secure.
- I want to be inspired by what I learn every day.
- When I am older, I want to do something that makes me feel safe and happy.
- I want to give back to others.

How does this list look to you? When you know your deepest desires, you naturally set intentions to make them happen.

Intentions help you focus your attention and actions on making desires happen. They give you the will—or the determination—to do certain things.

So if you want to feel healthy, you can say, "My intent is to feel healthy." Then ask yourself: *What can I do to make this happen?* Some possibilities include:

- I can eat healthy foods.
- I can drink lots of water.
- I can move my body.
- I can get at least eight to nine hours of sleep at night.

You have the power to make choices in your life to live your intentions.

Intentions are not about checking something off a list. They are also different from goals (like getting an A in math or winning a swim meet). Rather, intentions are

who you aspire to be as a person and what you want to contribute to your life and the lives of others.

For some intentions, you may not be sure what you can do to make them happen. That's okay. Just having the intention is the first, and most important, step.

Once you know your intentions, state them through a ritual. A ritual is a way of focusing your mind and your energy. You can write or draw your intent or say it out loud. There is a power in the ritual of saying your intent aloud or writing it down. This is a way that you can take responsibility for it. You may want to see your intent every day, or you may want to write or say it once and then let it go.

When you state your intent, naturally, with time, you will think of things you can do to live it in your life. Also, you will actively notice opportunities to engage with people or do new things to bring the energy of the intention into your life.

Intents change at different times in your life. Your intent right now may be to act nicely toward your sibling, and in the future, when you are a grown up, it may change to be a loving parent. Or your intent may be to do well in school, but in the future, it may evolve into being a good doctor to help heal others.

If you feel comfortable, you can share your intentions with loved ones. By telling even one trusted person what it is you truly want, and how you plan to make it happen, they can be there to support and motivate you to achieve your intent.

An intent is like a seed that we plant in the ground. We bury it in the soil, water it, and let the sun nurture it. With time, it blossoms into a beautiful tree or flower. Intentions are about your personal journey and how you want to lead a healthier, happier, more connected, and meaningful life.

EXERCISE:

SET AN INTENTION TODAY!

- - - - - - - - - - - -

Time Needed: **TEN MINUTES**

Location: **SOMEWHERE QUIET**

Materials Needed: **PAPER AND COLORED PENCILS
OR CRAYONS**

Sit comfortably.

Place one hand on your stomach and one hand on your heart.

Take a deep breath, in and out.

Choose one of the desires on page 36, or finish this sentence: "I want _____." (For example, "I want meaningful relationships with my family and friends.")

Based on the desire you chose, set an intention: "My intent is _____." (For example, you can say, "My intent is to be a good friend.")

As you breathe in and out again, let the words seep into your body, and feel what these words mean to you.

Take your paper and pencil or crayon, and write your intention: "My intent is _____."

Write it in a certain color, and/or draw it if you want to.

Now think of things you can do to live this intent. You can write these ideas down on the paper. If you don't have any ideas right now, that's fine. Just stating your intent is a good first step.

When you feel done, put the paper in front of you.

Place one hand on your stomach and one hand on your heart.

Looking at the piece of paper, take another deep breath, in and out.

You can choose what you do next. You can:

- *share your intent with someone you trust*
- *keep your paper in a private or public place*
- *throw your paper away*

Over the next week, every day, say your intent at least once to yourself. If it's helpful, you can do this with your hands on your heart and stomach to feel your intent as well. Notice if there are new opportunities for you to live your intent. For example, if your intent is to be a good friend, you might notice when you have some free time and call your friend to see how they are doing.

You can do this exercise over and over again. You can choose the same intent or a different intent listed on page 36. Or you can think of new intentions, ones that are important and meaningful to you!

What Words Describe Me?

• • • • •

Your character is how you and others describe the kind of person you are.

Think about these words: kind, generous, helpful, loving, supportive, thoughtful, articulate, confident. Now think about these words: nervous, insecure, angry, greedy, bossy.

Notice how some words seem to have positive qualities and others negative ones.

There are also words like these: quiet, loud, playful, serious. These words can describe positive or negative characteristics depending on the situation.

Words that you like, as well as words that you may dislike, describe a personality that is uniquely yours. Your words may change during the day or at different times of your life. For example, you may be a kind, supportive big sister, but you may also get angry when your little sister insists on playing with your favorite toys. You may feel confident telling stories to your parents, but when your teacher calls on you in class, you feel nervous.

The truth is that most people have parts of their personality that they are proud of and parts they want to improve.

Choosing words that define you can help you know yourself better and can also help you be the person you want to be.

> "The things that make me different are the things that make me ME."
> —PIGLET IN *WINNIE THE POOH*

Does Anyone See Me?

• • • • •

There are times when everyone feels as if no one sees or understands them. You may feel different, not normal, weird, misunderstood, alone, disliked, or ashamed of who you are or where you come from.

There are parts of you that are just who you are when you are born—your body, your skin color, your ethnicity. Then there are things that distinguish you—who and what you like, what you choose to do, how you communicate.

You have strengths and weaknesses like everyone. And you make mistakes like everyone too. Try to remember that you are special just the way you are.

People react differently when they feel that they are not being seen for who they really are. Some people decide to make sure they are seen by being loud or by acting boldly to get people's attention. Other people are quiet and try not to be noticed by others. And lots of people pretend to act in ways that they *think* others believe is cool. They do things to fit in, even though it doesn't feel right. They may do things to please others, even though they don't please themselves.

If you aren't being who you truly are—even if you please others—you won't feel at peace. You may find that you have more anxiety, can't sleep well, or fall into unhealthy habits.

It can be scary to express your true self, and sometimes it may even upset others, but when you do, you will feel honest and real. You will find that those who love you for who you really are will be the strongest champions who celebrate you!

There is a traditional greeting by the Zulu people in South Africa that honors the beauty and right to be seen for who a person is. When two people meet, they look at each other and say:

Sikhona, which means
I am here to be seen.

And then they reply:

Sawubona, which means
I see you.

Remember that you are worth being seen. You deserve to be seen.

When you feel lonely, misunderstood, or as if you don't fit in, one thing you can do is see someone else. Perhaps it is asking your teacher to tell you something about themselves. What is their favorite food? What are their hobbies? Or perhaps it is sitting with a classmate who usually sits alone at lunch and getting to know them. It could also even be volunteering somewhere safe with your family or classmates— maybe at a nursing home, where you might learn wisdom from those who have led amazing lives.

Seeing others in an honest and meaningful way helps you connect better with people. It also allows you to see the wonderful qualities in yourself.

What Do I Want?

43

EXERCISE:
I SEE YOU!

Time Needed: **A FEW SECONDS**
Location: **ANYWHERE**

Choose a partner for this exercise. It could be a sibling, friend, parent or relative, caretaker, or teacher (really, anyone in your life who is willing to try).

Over the next few days try different ways of greeting each other every time you meet. Here are some ideas:

Look at each other.

You say, "I am here to be seen." The other person says, "I see you."

Now switch. They say, "I am here to be seen." You say, "I see you."

Bow to each other.

In some Asian cultures, people bow to one another to show respect.

Put the palms of your hands together and place them in front of your heart.

In India, people use this gesture and say the word Namaste, *which means "I honor the divine in you."*

Hands to heart.

In Malaysia, after lightly holding each other's hand, people place a hand on their heart, look at each other, and nod.

Shake hands.

Take your right hand and hold the right hand of the other person. Give it a firm shake!

Air kiss.

Kiss the tips of your fingers and blow kisses to one another.

Cheek to cheek.

In some European and South American cultures, people do quick cheek-to-cheek greetings. Start with your right cheek to the other person's right cheek, and do a quick air kiss. Then put your left cheek to their left cheek and do another quick air kiss.

Hug.

A safe hug feels warm and comforting.

What Do I Want?

45

How Do I Deal with Disappointment?

· · · · ·

There will be times in life when you don't get something you want. Maybe it is not getting elected to student council or not being chosen to participate on a team. As you get older, it may be not being accepted into your dream college after you worked so hard in high school or not getting a job you really wanted.

You may also feel that someone else got something you really wanted because they had more money, had family advantages, are of a different race, or just got benefits that don't seem fair. The fact is things like this happen, and it is difficult to celebrate someone else's good news when you get bad news. Somehow you need to remember that lots of the causes of your disappointment are not about you—many systems in our society are unfair and discriminatory. (Think about how people have also dedicated their lives to change such systems.)

Disappointment can feel overwhelming. You can feel the anxiety in your body—your heart may feel broken and your stomach uneasy. You may feel lower back pain or stress in your shoulders. Your body takes on a lot of the emotional stress from disappointment.

When you are sad like this, there are several things you can do:

• Cry—you may just need to let out the tears!

• Talk—reach out to understanding people, whether they are friends, parents, siblings, or other family members or trusted adults.

• Hug—ask someone you trust to hug you.

• Exercise—when you move your body, you release stress and build up good hormones that make you feel better.

• Sleep—your body needs rest to recover from emotional stress.

• Expect the waves—you may cry, feel better, and then suddenly, the sad emotions come again. This is normal.

When you learn to live through your disappointments, you will become a stronger and more resilient person.

The most successful people in the world didn't let the word "no" stop them from going after what they wanted. They believed in their talents, their worth, and their voice and kept trying. Others point out that disappointments led them to explore new possibilities. And some feel that the rejection or failure of not getting what they thought they really wanted turned out to be a gift that inspired them to seek new opportunities and to find success in unexpected ways.

How Can I Feel Peaceful?

· · · · ·

There is a lot of noise in this world. And all the noise may make you feel overwhelmed and stressed out. You may feel:

- that you are bombarded with opinions, expectations, requests, and demands from others
- as if you aren't included in friend groups or teams you want to be a part of (you may see parties on social media or group chats and feel left out)
- upset by politics or that your parents are struggling with money
- nervous about safety in your school or community
- that you have too much homework or things to do, and just want to watch YouTube or play video games

You may just yearn to feel peaceful inside. If you feel peaceful inside, you will be more able to handle all the chaos and noise around you.

One way to feel peaceful inside is to become more comfortable with being quiet. When you are quiet while awake (not asleep!), you are more in touch with your thoughts, feelings, and body. You can then make decisions based on your own intuition and what feels right to you.

Many people are not used to being quiet. In fact, you may feel nervous being quiet because you are used to being surrounded by noise. Here are a few things you can try in order to get more used to being quiet:

Meditate.

- Begin by sitting in a quiet place. Take a deep breath, in and out. Try to take ten deep breaths like this and see how you feel.

Go for a quiet walk or run outside.

- You will still probably hear lots of noises, whether it is cars or people talking or construction. But go for a walk or run without headphones or music blasting. If you are with someone else, decide you both will be quiet and not talk. Breathe in the air around you.

Have a quiet meal.

• It's nice to have meals with friends and family because you can catch up on the day's events and share what is happening in your life.
Many people, however, get used to eating meals while watching television or doing work. Try to have a quiet meal—even shared with others—and appreciate the tastes, smells, look, and feel of the food you are eating. If not for the full meal, try it for the first five minutes at least.

Take time away from social media.

• Put your phone, if you have one, in another room. Decide not to watch YouTube or play video games. Let yourself be bored, even for five minutes. Maybe just sit in a room in your house or classroom and look around.

For a few minutes, feel what it is like to be a human BE-ing, not a human DO-ing.

By just BE-ing, you can feel the power of the quiet presence inside of you. You can take that peaceful quiet wherever you go and find it in the noisiest and busiest places you end up in.

What Symbols
Are Meaningful to Me?

• • • • •

An archetype is a symbol that represents something meaningful. An archetype can be a real person, a character, a shape, or a thing. Animals, objects in nature, and mythological characters have been common archetypes for thousands of years in cultures around the world.

Often you will see archetypes in art or stories—paintings, books, TV shows, movies, and video games. Think of a hero or villain, the fairy godmother, the jokester, a dog or dolphin, a tree or star, and then of how they come up in different ways in the stories you like most.

When you have archetypes in your life, they can give you comfort when you see or think about them. You can also use archetypes to remember how you *want* to feel, to treat others, or to act.

When you see a symbol, by chance or repeatedly, you can think about why you are seeing, or noticing, it. Maybe the symbol is trying to tell you something, like go slowly, try something different, or go after something you really want but may be nervous to pursue!

There are hundreds of archetypes, and they can have different meanings. How you chose to interpret them is up to you.

Below are a few examples to give you a sense of how popular archetypes are used in music, art, literature, and mythology.

Lioness

The female lion hunts for food and protects her children. She is fierce, strong, nurturing, and loving all at the same time.

Snake

The snake often represents rebirth because it sheds its skin and gets a new one as it grows. In ancient Egypt, the headdress of pharaohs (rulers) featured the snake and represented a connection to the divine in protection. In the Hebrew Bible of Judaism (the Old Testament of Christianity), the snake is in the Garden of Eden and can represent evil.

Dove

This white bird often represents hope and optimism. It is a symbol of peace.

Tree

A tree is old and rooted in the ground. It represents stability and wisdom.

Star

Stars have lasted forever and represent the eternal. They are also hopeful and magical, and bring light to the dark skies.

God of Love

In India, Krishna is the god of love, music, and compassion. In Roman mythology, Cupid played the same role.

Mother Goddess

In ancient Egypt, Isis was a protective mother and the goddess of the afterlife. Gaia in Greek mythology is the mother goddess of Planet Earth.

LION'S BREATH

- - - - - - - - - - - - - -

Time Needed: **ONE MINUTE**
Location: **ANYWHERE**

This breathing exercise is used in yoga to help stretch the muscles in your face, to let out energy, and to feel strong (and maybe a little silly!).

Sit cross-legged with your back straight.

Stretch both arms in front of your knees, with your hands open and fingers stretched.

Breathe in through your nose, filling up your lungs.

Open your mouth and stick your tongue out as far as you can. Try to keep your eyes wide open too!

Breathe out, making a loud "Aaaaaahhhh" sound (like the roar of a lion).

Bring your tongue back into your mouth, and breathe in normally through your nose.

In the beginning, try this one to two times. If comfortable, you can build up to ten lion's breaths. If you feel light-headed at any point, stop the exercise and just breathe normally.

Throughout the day, you can use this breath to get more energy or use it for motivation to feel strong and ready for any task!

HOW CAN I SERVE?

How Can I Serve?

· · · · ·

As you grow older, you will likely work to earn the material things to make you feel safe, secure, and happy. By being a good friend and family member, you will develop a community to support you and those you care about through difficult times and to celebrate milestones like birthdays, graduations, and weddings.

Often the richest moments in life come when you make a meaningful difference in someone else's life. When you help others, you receive the personal benefits of happiness and fulfilment that cannot be bought with money or material things.

There are different ways to think about service as you grow older. Ask yourself these questions:

· How can I serve myself?
(Remember: One of the best ways to take care of others
is to first take care of yourself.)

· How can I serve my loved ones, such as family and friends?

· How can I serve my community, which includes schools,
religious organizations, and my neighborhood?

· How can I serve my world, such as strangers,
animals, and the planet?

Now think about what you can do for each of these groups. When you serve others, you will feel that life has meaning and purpose.

Ways to serve could include:

· helping at home

· doing something nice for your neighbor

· teaching a younger sibling something that you are good at

· giving a compliment and making someone smile

· volunteering at a local organization

· collecting food or clothing to donate to a homeless shelter

As you think about your studies in school and what you want to do when you grow up, asking, "How can I serve?" can help you make choices to lead a full and meaningful life.

How Can I Take Care of Myself?

· · · · ·

The concept of well-being means being comfortable, healthy, and happy. There are scientists who study the well-being of people, companies, countries, and the world. The research on well-being shows that when you are happy, the people around you are also happy. When you pay attention to eating healthier foods, those around you may choose to consume healthier foods as well.

When you ask, "How can I serve myself?," you become a stronger person who can serve others. As you grow older, your well-being will adjust along with your body, interests, education, job, and where you live.

Some of the basics of well-being include:

- a place to live
- healthy food
- physical and emotional health
- financial security
- a secure job
- meaningful relationships
- feeling that what you do every day matters

If someone is thriving in all the areas above, they are very lucky. Most people in the world are struggling in some areas but are doing okay in others. Checking in on your well-being can help you live a better life. And knowing where you may be struggling can help you set intentions, ask for help, and make positive changes in your life.

EXERCISE:

MY WELL-BEING WHEEL

- - - - - - - - - - - - - -

Time Needed: **FIFTEEN MINUTES**
Location: **ANYWHERE**

Look at the following list:

- *Sleep*
- *Good Nutrition*
- *Exercise*
- *Family*
- *Friends*
- *School & Extracurricular Activities*
- *Fun*
- *Quiet Time*

There are ten questions on page 66. Before reading each question, take a deep breath, in and out.

After you read the question, notice how you feel as you answer the question.

Using a scale of 1-10, answer the question by choosing a number that feels right to you.

- *1-3: I am struggling!*
- *4-6: I am surviving!*
- *7-10: I am thriving!*

sleep

quiet
time

fun

good
nutrition

school +
extracurricular
activities

exercise

friends

family

Here are the questions:

1. *Do I sleep enough?*

2. *Do I eat healthy foods?*

3. *Do I move enough?*

4. *Do I have good relationships in my family?*

5. *Do I have one or two good friends?* (Note: the question isn't about the number of friends you have, but rather if you feel that you have at least one good friend who knows you.)

6. *Do I like what I am studying in school?*

7. *Do I try my best in school?*

8. *Do I like what I do outside of school?* (These include extracurricular activities like sports teams, martial arts, dance, art or music classes, etc.)

9. *Do I have enough fun every day?* (Maybe these overlap with extracurricular activities, but it could be reading for fun, playing video games, watching YouTube or TV shows, hanging out with friends, etc.)

10. *Do I have enough quiet time every day?* (Meaning to pray, to meditate, to be bored, to let your mind rest.)

On a piece of paper, write the numbers you felt while you looked at the questions. The challenge is to be honest with yourself and write what you felt the minute you asked the question.

As you get older, the questions you ask yourself will likely change. You may ask things like: "Do I like my job?" "Do I feel that I make enough money?" "Do I like where I live?"

How Can I Make Good Choices?

• • • • •

One of the most powerful tools you have in your life is the ability to reflect. Reflection means that you think back on your actions, moods, and thoughts after they have happened. When you reflect, you can see if you feel good or bad about something that happened and how you reacted to it. Here are some things you might reflect on:

• Perhaps you said something to someone that was hurtful. Upon reflection, you can make a choice to apologize.

• Perhaps you are really upset after your best friend posted a photo with someone else while at the mall. Upon reflection, you may realize it's okay for her to have other friends.

• Perhaps you aren't feeling good in your body today. Upon reflection, you can think back on what you ate yesterday. Maybe you had too much sugar, didn't exercise, spent too much time on your phone or computer, or didn't sleep enough. You can choose healthier habits today.

• Perhaps you didn't try your hardest on your math test and wish you had done better. Upon reflection, you can study harder next time or go to your teacher to ask for help.

• Perhaps you see that someone sits by themselves every day at lunch at school. Upon reflection, you can choose to reach out to them and invite them to eat with you and your friends.

• Perhaps you did something that you are ashamed of and are scared someone will find out about. Upon reflection, you may realize that it is better to reach out to a trusted adult or good friend to help you admit what you did instead of living with fear and guilt.

• Perhaps you said something rude to your mom when she dropped you off at the bus this morning. Upon reflection, you can tell her you love her when you get home.

Reflection helps make you a smarter, stronger, and kinder person. It helps you learn, adjust, and change things to make you happier and healthier. Reflection helps you make better choices every day for yourself and those around you.

EXERCISE:

WHAT DID I DO YESTERDAY?

Time Needed: **FIFTEEN MINUTES**
Location: **SOMEWHERE QUIET**

In this exercise, you are going to replay in your mind everything that happened to you yesterday. Think of it as watching yourself in a movie. As you watch yourself and remember what happened, pay attention to how you feel during the highlight moments. Think about the choices you made and if they feel right to you today as you replay them.

Sit comfortably.

Put away any electronics and turn your phone on silent.

Take a deep breath. In and out. Another breath. In and out.

In your mind, let's begin with the morning and ask some questions:

- *How did you wake up? Think about how you felt that moment you woke up—rested or did you want to sleep more? Did you remember your dreams when you woke up?*

- *What is your morning routine? Did you do it yesterday? Did you brush your teeth or wash your face first? Did you choose your clothes, or were they already laid out? What did you wear yesterday?*

- *Did you eat something before heading out for the day? What did you eat? Where did you eat it? What conversations did you have?*

How Can I Serve?

69

Now play out the rest of your day:

- If you went to school, replay the conversations with friends, teachers, and/or administrators. What classes did you have? Did you learn anything new or exciting?
- If you didn't go to school, play out your other activities of the day.

Be as specific as possible when replaying these moments:

- See yourself eating lunch, snacks, and dinner.
- How did you wind down at the end of the day? What did you wear to go to sleep?
- Did you brush your teeth and wash your face? Did you follow the same routine you do every night?

See yourself lying in bed before falling asleep. Take a deep, conscious breath again. In and out.

How did this day feel to you?

Go back to any moments that stood out to you—moments in which you may have felt happy or sad, frustrated or excited, full of joy or sadness. Reflect on how you reacted, and right now take a moment to appreciate or learn from them.

Take a deep breath. In and out.

Think about any actions or words you may have done differently now that you've reflected on them. Is there anything you can do or say tomorrow to make you feel better? Is there anything you can learn for future situations?

How Can I Be Kind?

· · · · ·

Kindness is the act of doing something for someone else to make them feel happy. When you do something kind, you don't expect anything back. You just do it because you want to.

You can be kind to someone you love or to a stranger. You can be kind through your thoughts, with your words, or through your actions.

Kindness may be as simple as:

- saying good morning to your bus driver
when you head to school
- telling the postal worker thank you when she drops off
a package at your house
- congratulating your classmate
who won the school election
- praising your parent's outfit
- sharing your cookie with your friend
- inviting the new kid at school to sit with you
and your friends at lunch
- shoveling snow for your elderly neighbor
- volunteering for a beach cleanup on the weekend

When you do something kind and mean it from the very bottom of your heart, you may find that you feel really good about yourself! In fact, when you are feeling sad or lonely, doing something kind for someone else can be the best way to change your mood.

> The American author Mark Twain said, "Kindness is a language which the deaf can hear and the blind can see."

EXERCISE:

ACTS OF KINDNESS FOR MYSELF AND OTHERS

Time Needed: **ONE MINUTE**
Location: **ANYWHERE**

Sit comfortably.

Place your hand on your heart and take a deep breath, in and out.

Ask yourself, What is one thing I can do to be kind to myself? *Decide what you are going to do and when you will do it.*

Ask yourself, What is one thing I can do to be kind to someone else? *Decide what you are going to do and when you will do it.*

What Do I Like to Do?

• • • • •

Each one of us has natural things we like doing. These could be:

- speaking or performing in front of others
- organizing activities with your friends
- assigning roles on your robotics team
- drawing really well and conveying ideas through cool pictures
- excelling at math and thinking about statistics
for your favorite sports team to win a game
- fixing or building things
- reading a lot and answering people's questions
when they turn to you for facts or knowledge
- getting people to understand and forgive each other

You may call what you like doing a strength, because it is easy and effortless for you. However, it is really important to remember that you can also cultivate things that don't come easily to you and turn them into strengths. Research shows that you can always improve skills, and in fact, your brain grows and strengthens when you struggle, persist, and work hard. But remember to try to distinguish what comes easy for you from what gives you joy.

When you know what you enjoy doing, you can use your skills to help yourself and others. As you grow older, if you find roles in which you are doing things that make you happy—in school, in your community, or one day at your job—you can serve others and be more successful.

You can also think about how to build teams. You can learn how to work with others who compliment your skills. For example, if you love to write, you might find someone who likes to draw well or who can manage the numbers for a future project that will allow everyone to be more successful. As you grow older, learning how to bring your joyful passions to a team is a powerful skill to have.

Who Are My Heroes?

· · · · ·

Heroes are people in your community or in our world who are admired for their courage or achievements. Through their words and actions, heroes lead by example and show ways in which we can make the world a better place.

Heroes can be people in your neighborhood—like the firefighter who puts their life in danger to help others or the principal of your school who makes sure that all the students have access to a good education. Heroes, like everyone else, have strengths and weaknesses. They are real people with feelings and insecurities. They have friends and family, and sometimes their sacrifices hurt those they love. Often some of the most well-known heroes suffered tremendously, made mistakes, and had regrets. Heroes also often have resilience—the ability to get back up when they have been knocked down.

Heroes believe in something bigger than themselves, and this drives them to fight for what they believe in. They are willing to sacrifice themselves and their well-being for others.

Remembering that heroes are only human, you can learn a lot from them. You can explore the issues they fought for, and you can adopt the qualities in them that you admire.

Here are some popular heroes you may want to learn more about:

• *Mother Teresa* was a Catholic nun who helped children in need in India. She is often respected for her love, sacrifice, and commitment to the poor.

• *Rosa Parks* is a civil rights hero, often known for not moving her seat on a segregated bus in Montgomery, Alabama. She had a long history of fighting for people's rights even before she became famous.

• *Albert Einstein* was a brilliant mathematician who created the theory of relativity in science. He was a genius.

• *Michelangelo* was a great painter, sculptor, scientist, and inventor.

• *Harvey Milk* was a gay activist in San Francisco, California. He was the first openly gay person elected to public office.

• *Florence Nightingale* cared for the sick during war times and transformed the profession of nursing.

• *Mahatma Gandhi* believed in nonviolent protest and was the symbol of India when it won freedom from colonial Britain. He inspired other heroes like *Martin Luther King Jr.*, who championed civil rights in the United States, and *Nelson Mandela*, who sacrificed decades of his life to fight apartheid in South Africa and who became the country's first president.

• *Helen Keller* was deaf and blind, and she became the first person with those disabilities to graduate from college.

• *Jane Goodall* has spent her life studying gorillas to help save the species. She is an animal activist.

• *Greta Thunberg* is a teenage activist who is bringing attention to the climate change crisis and calling for international action.

• *Malala Yousafzai* is an activist for human rights and education, particularly for girls. She is the youngest person to win the Nobel Peace Prize.

What Can I Do
to Take Care of the Planet?

• • • • •

Our planet is often referred to as Mother Earth. In cultures around the world, mothers work, take care of children, feed their communities, and are beacons of love and safety. Most of us wish for a nurturing mother who can take care of us, encourage us, and help us achieve our dreams. In the same way, we wish that our planet—our Mother Earth—will be able to provide us with safety, shelter, food, and stability.

The planet is like our body. The trees are like our lungs, providing us with the oxygen to live. The rivers and oceans are like our circulation, moving and keeping us fresh and vital.

Mother Earth is suffering. Global warming is affecting our water, soil, land, and air. Animals are suffering too, and certain species are endangered or almost extinct. You may be experiencing extreme hot or cold weather, rains, floods, fires, hurricanes, tornadoes, and other disasters where you live. Environmental factors may be influencing how you feel or the health of someone you love. You may live in a city that has terrible air pollution or where you must be careful of the water that you drink.

As you grow older, it is likely that the health of Mother Earth may affect many of your decisions. Sadly, we are all living in a time where we can no longer take the stability of our planet for granted. But there are several things you can do to help Mother Earth right now:

• Educate yourself about global warming. As you grow older,
you will hear more about the state of our planet, and you may find
that people have different points of view on the subject.
You will be empowered in these conversations if you know your facts.
Your teachers and librarians can probably help you find good books
on the topic that are easy to understand.

• Ask your parents and other adults how they interact with the environment.
Do they consider the planet when making decisions?
Why or why not?

• Be a good planetary citizen. Recycle.
Avoid using plastic bottles and wasting paper.

EXERCISE:

WHAT CAN I DO FOR WHERE I LIVE?

Time Needed: **AS MUCH AS YOU WANT**
Location: **A QUIET PLACE TO BRAINSTORM AND ALSO A PLACE IN YOUR COMMUNITY**
Materials Needed: **A PIECE OF PAPER AND PENCIL**

Thinking about the planet's health can be overwhelming. But coming up with one way that you can serve Mother Earth can be impactful and fulfilling.

If possible, find a quiet place outside to brainstorm. Perhaps it's sitting on a bench in a park or in your neighborhood, lying on the grass in your backyard, or sitting in the sand by the beach or on the banks of a local pond or river.

Take a deep breath, in and out.

Look around you and appreciate what the planet offers you.

Notice the grass, water, trees, bushes, or flowers that surround you.

Look up at the sky. Notice the color of the sky and the clouds above.

Feel the heat of the sun.

Breathe in the air. Breathe out.

Now think of one thing you can do where you live to serve Mother Earth.

Perhaps it is planting seeds for flowers or some vegetables in your backyard or in a pot for your apartment.

Or maybe you could clean up your sidewalk, a local park, or a part of the beach.

Create posters to encourage people to recycle plastic bottles and hang them around places where lots of people will see them, like a downtown area.

Write postcards to local leaders to support an environmental law that you believe in.

Think about the people you can ask to join you in doing this one thing for Mother Earth. Commit to asking them to support you, but be resolute to do what you want to do no matter what.

Commit to helping others do what they want to do to help the environment.

Remember: it doesn't have to be a huge action, just one thing to support the planet.

WHAT AM I
GRATEFUL FOR?

Who Am I Grateful For?

• • • • •

Think about the people in your life who take care of, teach, inspire, and love you.
These people may include:

• your parents, grandparents,
siblings, cousins, or other family members

• teachers who spend long days preparing
and teaching you at school

• coaches who train you to be mentally
and physically fit

• social workers who come and
check up on you

• friends and teammates
who you spend time with

• musicians, dancers, poets, or actors
who entertain and inspire you

When you are feeling down, discouraged, or alone, making a conscious effort to think about people in the world who have made you smile can help you change your mood and feel more connected with life and others.

EXERCISE:

EXPRESS YOUR GRATITUDE

- - - - - - - - - - - -

Time Needed: **TEN MINUTES**
Location: **SOMEWHERE PRIVATE OR A SAFE SPACE WITH OTHERS
WHERE YOU FEEL FREE TO SPEAK HONESTLY**
Materials Needed: **TWO CHAIRS**

In this exercise, you are going to express your gratitude and appreciation for someone else. Since sometimes it is hard to tell someone directly how you feel, you are going to speak to them while imagining that they are there.

Place two chairs facing each other.

Sit in one chair. (This will be chair 1.)

Take a deep breath, in and out.

Place a hand on your heart and think about someone you are grateful for.

Imagine this person sitting in the chair in front of you. (This will be chair 2.)

Now tell this person (even though you are only imagining them) why you appreciate and are grateful for them. You can say as much as you want to say.

Now switch chairs.

Sit in chair 2 and imagine that you are the person you were talking to. You can sit the way they sit, move the way they would move, and listen as they would listen.

Imagine looking at yourself in chair 1 and hearing the words of gratitude you just uttered.

Being the person in chair 2, appreciate these words. Then say thank you to yourself in chair 1.

What Are My Favorite Holidays?

· · · · ·

Holidays are usually times when people reflect, pray, remember, or celebrate something. Holidays around the world are often celebrated with music and dance, new clothes, presents, decorating homes, and lots of food. Often family and friends gather together on holidays.

For some people, such gatherings may create anxiety because there are disagreements between family and friends. And yet many people still choose to participate in holiday traditions because it is personally meaningful or important to loved ones.

Thinking about your favorite holidays, and why they make you happy, is a powerful way to feel grateful for your family, culture, religion, and country.

Perhaps you look forward to Christmas every year, because your family travels from around the world to share meaningful gifts with one another.

Or maybe you enjoy Holi, the festival of color, where people dance and throw powdered colors to friends and neighbors.

Maybe the month of Ramadan grounds you in prayer and contemplation every year, and you look forward to breaking the fast with your family each night.

Perhaps you look forward to Carnival and the dancing and singing in the streets of your city.

Maybe you enjoy Juneteenth instead of Independence Day.

Learning about holidays in other cultures and countries is also a wonderful way to appreciate the diversity of traditions around the world. While holidays may be very different for your friends from other cultures, taking interest in them can also help you see how so many people around the world appreciate family and community on these special days.

What Inspires Me?

• • • • •

Many English words are made up of Latin or Greek roots, or represent ideas from others words. "Inspire" is such a word. See how it is made up of two parts: "in" and "spirit." When you are inspired, you are connected to your spirit. "Spirit" may mean different things to different people. It may mean a connection to God or to creativity or to your soul.

When you are inspired, you may find that you have a new, exciting, or brilliant idea. You might feel energy to do something and feel hopeful and full of life.

Part of your life journey is figuring out what inspires you—what makes you feel fully alive, creative, and joyful!

Things that may inspire you are:

- music
- art
- words
- movement
- animals
- nature

When you are inspired, time may feel as if it is standing still, it is endless, and you can do whatever you are doing without any worries.

You may feel inspired while:

- building a city with Legos or in Minecraft—
  you create with imagination and freedom

- playing your trumpet and getting lost in the notes—
  you don't even need to try; the music just comes

- cuddling with your new puppy—
  you don't feel any judgement, just love and comfort

- playing basketball with friends at the park—
  you go into a zone, seeing the ball swoosh into the hoop with no effort

Take a moment, right now, to think about those times when you don't worry about time or how you perform or what others think about you. Think about what inspires you most in the world to be you best, happiest self.

Gratitude for Life Itself!

· · · · ·

Life is an adventure that has ups and downs.

Suffering is part of the human experience. You will face disappointment. You will make mistakes. You will be embarrassed and ashamed at times. You will feel lonely and lost, and you may go through stretches of dark times when it is hard to see the light. You will cry and feel grief.

Part of being human is the ability to survive and thrive in different situations. There are people who are suffering from poverty, hunger, captivity, war, abuse, and many other unfair injustices. Often, though, we can turn to these people for inspiration on how to get through difficult times and to live with dignity.

Experiencing joy, creativity, love, and inspiration are also part of BE-ing human.

Think of standing in a hallway with a flashlight. To get to your destination, you point the flashlight in the direction you are walking, only seeing the path that the light shows to get where you are supposed to go.

You can approach life a bit differently with the tools of reflection, intention, self-discovery, and flexibility. Think what your journey would be like if you had a larger flashlight that showed you there are rooms along the hallway. You *can* wander from the straight path.

With more light, you may notice that you are in a museum, with rooms full of treasures you never saw before. You can keep discovering new things, exploring new corners of the many rooms that have opened up to you. And maybe one day, the lights come on, and you are immersed in absolute magic!

There will be hard times in everyone's life. But if you can find moments every day to seek out joy, you can feel gratitude for life itself. Take risks and explore those dark rooms. Smile, connect with someone you love, listen to a beautiful piece of music, or just dance freely with no one watching you.

Every day, remind yourself, *I am lucky and grateful to be alive.*

EXERCISE:

WHAT GIVES ME JOY?

- - - - - - - - - - - - - -

Time Needed: **TEN MINUTES FOR EACH STEP**
Location: **ANYWHERE**
Materials Needed: **PAPER AND PEN**

The goal of this exercise is to list the things that make you happy. The ritual of writing and seeing these words on paper will remind you that there are people, things, and activities that give you joy.

Step 1

Look at the mind map on the next page. You can copy it onto a piece of paper.

Now take a deep breath. In and out.

Place your hand on your heart. Smile.

In the bubbles, write the names of people, pets, places, activities, and objects that make you happy.

Write whatever comes to mind. Don't overthink any words. Be honest and fill in as many bubbles as you can.

When you think you are done, take another conscious breath, in and out.

Step 2

The next step is to think of things you can do to bring joy into your life. You can do this right now or come back to it in a few days.

Look at your mind map.

If you want to add more things to it, go ahead and add more bubbles and words.

Connect two bubbles on your map with a line. For example, if in one bubble you have written "food" and in another bubble you have written "friends," draw a line connecting them both.

Think of something you can do that involves "food" and "friends." For example, maybe it can be a playdate with a friend where you bake cookies together.

Connect other bubbles. See how many activities you can come up with.

The more random the connections, the more challenging and fun it will be to come up with activities.

You can place this map somewhere that reminds you there are many things in your life that give you joy. And when you need to do something to lift your mood, look at the activities you brainstormed, and take action by doing one of them!

What Did It Take for This Moment to Happen?

· · · · ·

Let's think about how many things need to happen for you to be reading this book just now.

It began with an intent—an intent on my part to create a book for kids to know that you are special.

Then, it took ideas. As an author, I am so lucky to be able to share my ideas with you through my words. My ideas come from my family, my teachers, the many books I have read, research from scientists, and thousands (millions!) of other people who influenced them.

I write words on a computer. Think of all the ideas and (millions!) of people who make it possible for us to work on computers. Think of all the materials it needs to make a computer—the keyboard, the screen, the hardware inside. And the software, which is the product of more ideas that make things happen.

A publisher—a company that makes books—has a team of people who put the book together. An editor checks grammar and makes sure the ideas make sense. An art director thinks about how the words can come to life through illustrations and then finds the illustrator who draws the pictures you see on these pages. The illustrator has dozens of people who have influenced her and who have helped her perfect her talent.

There are also the people who physically make the book. They figure out which paper to use, where to buy it from, and how to organize materials for the printer.

If you go back a step, you can think about the trees that the paper came from. Think about the seeds, the sun, the rain, and the time it took for that tree to grow. Think about what it took for that tree to be made into paper and who made the printing machines. Thousands of people and nature, itself, are part of this journey too.

There are sales people who find bookstores, libraries, clubs, and schools that want to carry the book and make it available to kids to read. And all this needs to be managed by business people who think about the expenses, how to pay everyone, and how to collect money to keep the publishing company and author successful.

Truck drivers take the books to warehouses, where they are then delivered to their next stop. Think about all the people—and all the ideas—that are needed to make trucks and warehouses.

Perhaps a parent or teacher decided to buy this book for you or your classmates. Or maybe you saw this book on a shelf in a library and were interested in looking at it.

So right now, as you look at this page, pause.

Take a deep breath. In and out.

Feel gratitude in your heart for the tangled web—all the ideas and people—that made this very moment possible.

What Do I See
When I Look at a Flower?

. . . . .

Buddha was a teacher who lived in India more than 2,500 years ago. He helped people see the world differently. People would come to visit him from distant lands to hear his words, to be inspired, to find comfort in their suffering, and to understand their purpose in life.

One day, over a hundred people gathered around Buddha in the forest for one of his famous lectures. Buddha picked up a flower and held it up in front of him. He looked at the flower and turned back to the people. His students waited for his words to inspire them. But he just held up the flower.

Finally, Ananda, one of his favorite students, bowed to the Buddha and smiled. The Buddha smiled lovingly back at him, gave him the flower, and left.

The crowd was bewildered. They gathered around Ananda, wondering what had just happened and why the Buddha had left them with no lesson.

Ananda asked them, "What did you see?"

"Just a flower," they all responded.

Ananda replied:

**I saw colors and smelled the scent
of the sweet rose.**

**I saw the seed that it came from, that travelled
through time to find its place in the ground.**

**I felt the warmth of the sun and the night skies
glittering with all the other stars in the galaxies.**

I saw the clouds and the sky, the rains and rainbows.

I saw the earth, and the insects that feed the soil.

I saw birds singing and bees making their honey.

**I saw children sweetening their food with honey, and
couples marrying with beautiful flowers around them.**

I saw love.

I saw myself and could not help but smile.

Those in the crowd realized that using just their eyes, they had only seen a flower. But Buddha had taught them how to see the whole universe in that one tiny flower. They saw themselves as the sun and stars, the soil, the rain, and all that made the flower a beautiful, nurturing symbol of love.

They knew that they were part of a universe that was always there to support them.

Remember: you are part of a larger universe. You reflect the sun, moon, stars, and galaxies. You are part of infinite stories, generations of ancestors, and rich experiences that made you, you.

And you are part of a story that will continue for eternity!

> "To see the world in a grain of sand and heaven in the wild flower, hold infinity in the palm of your hand and eternity in an hour."
> —WILLIAM BLAKE

I AM EVERYWHERE

Time Needed: **FIVE MINUTES**
Location: **INSIDE A ROOM**

Chose a comfortable chair, your bed, or a space on the floor where you can sit and feel at ease.

With your eyes open, look around you. Notice what is in the room: the furniture, other objects, and how the walls create a space around you.

If you are comfortable, close your eyes.

Being still in your body, as you are breathing, put your attention on your body. Feel how it exists in this space. Notice how your body feels on the chair, and feel how it is heavier than the air around you.

Try to watch yourself on this chair, almost as if you are someone else in the room taking a video of you, sitting in stillness, breathing in and out.

With a deep breath, in and out, put your attention on the you that is feeling your body.

You can imagine this by thinking of the air you are breathing as a light blue color. See this blue coming in and out of you with each breath.

As you breathe in and out, see this beautiful blue spreading into the space around you. With each breath, feel that lightness of being filling the space between your heavy body and the objects around you.

Let the blue stretch out to the walls that create the space of the room that you are sitting in. Imagine the blue, light and free, filling all the space around you, keeping you warm and safe and holding you.

Now let that blue spread beyond the walls of this room. With each breath, in and out, see the blue spread and spread—to other rooms beyond this room, beyond the walls, and to the world outside.

See the color spreading to the trees and flowers and grass outside.

In your mind, imagine something familiar outside, like your favorite tree.

Let the blue go to the tree and surround it with its comforting color.

With a breath in and out, see the blue go inside your tree. Feel your energy, the you that is this light blue, nurturing the tree, going deep into its core and down into the earth below.

Take a deep breath, in and out, for your tree.

Let the blue now come back up through the tree and stretch into branches and leaves and burst out into the space around the tree.

See the blue go up and up and up, beyond the clouds and into the sky above.

Feel your color spreading, getting lighter and darker, maybe even changing colors as it spreads everywhere.

See your blue color go out into the galaxy—into the stars you see at night. Feel the blue go inside a star, and breathe in and out, feeling you in that star.

Feel how you are now in all the space that exists, inside and outside of you, inside and outside of everything else: from the cells of your body to the trees, the stars, and entire universe.

AFTERWORD
BY DEEPAK CHOPRA

The purpose of life is the expansion of happiness. Every time you envision a goal, whatever that might be—healthy relationships, long life, business success, creative expression, joyful energy, self-esteem, higher consciousness—the underlying intention is always to be happy.

In the Eastern wisdom traditions, the path to enlightenment is the freedom from the conditioned mind. The conditioned mind is the hypnosis of social conditioning, which makes 99 percent of people in the world behave like biological robots, triggered by people and circumstances into predictable outcomes. The creative people of the world are the disruptors. They have stopped being reactive, biological robots and have tapped into fundamental creativity. Fundamental creativity is at the level of being.

All experience starts with the highest level of intelligence, which is being. Being is the source of thought, but also the source of feeling, thinking, reflecting, speaking, sensing, perceiving, and imagination. At the level of being, every human is a field of pure possibility, pure love, and pure creativity, and this automatically leads to success and fulfilment in all areas of life. Life unfolds in the following sequence: being, feeling, reflecting and thinking, speaking, and doing (taking action in the world).

Mallika's book reflects how you, as a conscious being, can be in touch with your own deeper self beyond your conditioned mind. It offers very practical ways and means to get in touch with aspects of your own being. It is simple and straightforward not only for kids but also for parents. If you follow the exercises and ideas in this book, you have the ticket to the freedom needed beyond the mind to create your own reality. This is the kind of education we want for all our children and in all our schools—instead of focusing on information overload, for which I would recommend Google, the priority should be self-reflection, happiness, and being of service to humanity.

Deepak Chopra

RESOURCES

Much of the content in this book comes from lifelong learning and exploration.

In particular, my father, Deepak Chopra, has championed mind, body, and spiritual concepts his entire life, and I am the beneficiary of endless conversations on the nature of consciousness. Two of his books were particularly relevant while I wrote this book:

The Soul of Leadership: Unlocking Your Potential for Greatness

The Seven Spiritual Laws of Success: A Practical Guide to the Fulfillment of Your Dreams

Other books that were influential while writing *Just Be You* include:

StrengthsFinder 2.0 by Tom Rath

Limitless Mind: Learn, Lead, and Live Without Barriers by Jo Boaler

Quiet: The Power of Introverts in a World That Can't Stop Talking by Susan Cain

Learned Hopefulness: The Power of Positivity to Overcome Depression by Dan Tomasulo

The Book of Symbols: Reflections on Archetypal Images by the Archive for Research in Archetypal Symbolism

ACKNOWLEDGMENTS

My family story shapes who I am. All of the things I write about in my books are influenced by the lessons my parents, Rita and Deepak Chopra, taught me.

My parents immigrated to the United States when they were in their early twenties so my father could train to be a doctor. I was born a year after they got here. During my childhood, I watched my parents work hard to build a life for my brother and me. They made many sacrifices to make sure we were well educated and had opportunities to pursue our dreams.

That spirit continues still. My mother is my biggest supporter and has taken care of my children since they were born. My father is the first person to read everything I write, gives me feedback, and is always willing to promote my work. I believe that the privilege I have as their daughter affords me the opportunity to ask, "How can I serve?"

I am incredibly grateful for my parents and strive to support my girls on their journeys of self-discovery and contribution just as my parents have supported me.

ALSO AVAILABLE FROM MALLIKA CHOPRA AND RUNNING PRESS KIDS:

Available wherever books and ebooks are sold!